What's It All About Nesheba?

What's It All About Nesheba?

Book Collection Series

Books Series 1-3

What's It All About Nesheba?
Purpose of the Journey
Book Series 1

What's It All About Nesheba?
Ever Evolving
Book Series 2

What's It All About Nesheba?
Pressing On...
Book Series 3

By. Nesheba

Essential Spirit Enterprises, Inc. – Inspirations
Self-Published via Lulu.com

Inspirations: What's It All About Nesheba? Book Collection Series

ISBN: 978-0-6152-4029-9

Library of Congress Control Number: 2008934964

Scriptures referenced throughout this book via chapter, verse, and footnotes from ILumina Gold Premium Software version utilizing the King James Version. Published by Tyndale House ©2006 – 2007 All Rights Reserved

American Psychological Association (APA):

strongholds. (n.d.). *The American Heritage® Dictionary of the English Language, Fourth Edition.* Retrieved January 15, 2008, from Dictionary.com website: http://dictionary.reference.com/browse/strongholds *All Rights Reserved*

Chicago Manual Style (CMS):

strongholds. Dictionary.com. *The American Heritage® Dictionary of the English Language, Fourth Edition.* Houghton Mifflin Company, 2004. http://dictionary.reference.com/browse/strongholds (accessed: January 15, 2008) *All Rights Reserved*

Modern Language Association (MLA):

"strongholds." *The American Heritage® Dictionary of the English Language, Fourth Edition.* Houghton Mifflin Company, 2004. 15 Jan. 2008. Dictionary.com http://dictionary.reference.com/browse/strongholds *All Rights Reserved*

Images used throughout this book are from: *All Rights Reserved*

Lulu.com – Market Place: http://www.lulu.com/

- John Gissy - The Power of Christ *All Rights Reserved*

- Ep Studiios & ESpiriteE: Book Cover Design *All Rights Reserved*

Free Digital Photos: http://freedigitalphotos.net/ Used by permission *All Rights Reserved*

- butterfly3
- 1_falls-of-shin
- 1_kilt-rock-waterfall
- sky5
- waterfall1
- fireworks
- sky1
- sunset23
- sunset25

What's It All About Nesheba? –
Series Collection...

Book 1-3 for Series 1-3

By Nesheba

✠✠✠

Table of Contents

❈ ❈ ❈
Preface

Hello one and all my name is Diahann a.k.a. writing under the name of Nesheba. I pray and hope you enjoy reading What's It All About Book Nesheba? Book Collection Series by Nesheba.

I've had an interesting journey along the way and wanted to share some of the revelations and thoughts experienced. Experiences, that caused me to pause at this juncture to reflect on all my gifts, trials & tribulations, and the overall direction for my life.

A majority of my professional experience is within IT / Telecommunications. I've been a team lead, technical support analyst, business analyst, and project manager. This is an industry I truly enjoy and have learned a lot from. Additionally, I also believe it's one of my gifts. This gift is shared via *Essential Spirit Enterprises, Inc.*, please feel free to visit: *http://www.espirite.net*

My life's journey and revelations lead me to the What's It All About Nesheba? Book Collection Series the releasing of my first gift writing. So, at this time I'd like to share that with you.

God has been a central part of my life and has been the answer to all that I've been through. I know in my heart I would have never made it this far without God, Jesus, and the Holy Spirit being in my life. I can't say it enough how much I pray these words help make your day brighter and assist you with your journey...

Thank you, for taking the time to enjoy and become inspired by these revelations...

What's It All About Nesheba?
Book Collection Series website is:
http://stores.lulu.com/eSpirite8Inspirations

Thank you, and Have a Blessed
& Peaceful Day!!!

What's It All About Nesheba? –
Purpose of the Journey...

Book 1 of Series 1

By Nesheba

❋❋❋

Table of Contents

1

❄❄❄

Purpose of the Journey

This day Sunday, December 31, 2006 the last day of the year, I sit hear ready to share a journey... A journey that began some years ago far away... Before conception ··· HE KNEW US {God sent the angel to confirm the birth of Jesus thereby knowing him before he was conceived. {KJV · Luke 2:21}...

Our journey whether short or long is planned by God... When we arrive, if we arrive the journey begins with revelation. Now, revelation and the discernment there of is the why we are here, and how we are to fore fill our purpose is the journey...

The sooner we discern the purpose those special gifts things we enjoy that come naturally in lay our treasures...Now these gifts that lead to our treasures are Blessed by God {{KJV - Job 22:25, Luke 12:34}. The greatest treasure and most precious are to know God, Jesus, and the Holy Spirit. Our greatest gift is to KNOW LOVE {KJV - 1 Corinthians 13:13}. AGAPE is unconditional love that surpasses all understanding, but by knowing this type of LOVE we can know God we can KNOW HIS HEART...

Knowing God is the most important part of the journey for without this knowledge {my people perish for a lack of knowledge {KJV – Hosea 4:6}. Although, love is the greatest gift of all God blesses us with an array of gifts. These gifts allow us to work, and have businesses to share our gifts with the world...

As you read these words of encouragement I pray that they reveal Gods Love and purpose for your life. In addition, I pray that these words go to the deepest part of you the place that only you & God know to nurture and feed your spirit, soul / mind and body. 'For greater is He that lives within me than he that lives within the world'. [1 John 4:4}.'

Additionally, I pray that you hold fast to these words 'I can do all things through Christ Jesus who strengthen me' {KJV - Philippians 4:13}. No matter what trials and tribulations we experience hold on to knowing Gods is with you always, and HE LOVES you just as you are...

The purpose of the journey is to know God and by knowing God you will come to know who you are and why HE brought you here at such a time as this...

Have you ever wondered why you where born during this time and season? Are you suppose to do something special? God knows the timing and season in which to bring us into the world to begin our journey. He even supplies us with natural tools to help get us through, but we aren't always readily aware of why. If you've noticed we also tend to gravitate to certain fields, places, and people, why is that? We don't always know why we just seem to go with the flow with questions we tend to hold within.

Exploring those thoughts that we hold within is apart of the journey releasing them is the revelation. Don't be afraid to venture within its like peeling away at an onion there's one layer after the other, and sometimes you might even cry. But, taking the chance to go on this exploration can become the most rewarding thing you've ever done in your life.

So, reach out to yourself, place yourself on the list everyone else is already there move yourself to the top of the list. Go for it, ride the wind, fly to the highest heights, run towards it like you need to save your life. Whatever you do don't be afraid of it embrace it.

It's can also be like climbing a mountain seeming ever impossible, ever so big, so rocky, never ending, but the joy of reaching the top despite all odds shows you can do anything if you put your heart and mind to it.

Sometimes we give up to easy because things get a little crazy, scary, the infamous fear of the unknown. Push hard and fast past these feelings and find the eagle from within by keeping your head to the sky. Allow the strength from within to be your friend this friend is the Holy Spirit within, the very presence of God, the quiet voice from within.

Feel the peace, feel the love, embrace it all and know that it's God who will always acknowledge your path towards the journey. Keep the peace, stay calm take this spiritual journey it will never let you down...

Never forget God is always with you I just can't say that enough, maintain your confidence even when at times you may think he isn't He's always present. He will never leave you nor forsake you....

I will and have prayed that this book collection series will assist you along the way, will bring a sense of comfort, will bring you peace, and will bring a sense of knowing everything will be alright...

Enjoy and relax while your read this series, mediate on the words may they feed your spirit and soul and bring you peace...

Road Towards the Journey

How long is this Journey, is it short or long?
What awaits us through the journey tears or joy?
If tears, joy comes in the morning
Whether short or long can we tell the story...?
Will the story say what we learned along the
way...?
Or will it say we continued the same road never
realizing,
Never knowing...

Knowing that along the way there are gifts of
wisdom to hold near and dear.
Taking that wisdom as a seed of love from God
To plant more seeds along the way to help shorten
the journey for ourselves and others,
Gifts to pass along the way...

Now, let me be clear trials, tribulations and
suffering although painful bring
us closer to God. Know HE has great blessings
waiting and that
the end of suffering is near...

This may seem strange but sometimes when
things are going well we may forget to Thank God
along the way.
Those that know God and HIS word are aware
that HE fore warned us
that trials will come but count it all joy...

Do you know if you can shorten your journey or
will it be long?
The journey isn't always long because of you,
sometimes the ones around
whom we love just can't get it clear...
If you see or discern this take it to God in prayer
and ask HIM to reveal
to those near and dear...
When they give you a window to share a word of
encouragement
walk through it to assist them in shortening their
journey.
The sooner they can discern their purpose
it will help things along the way...

Know that the closest to you friends, family or foe
are the ones that can be
hardest on us towards reaching our journey to
know...
Those of us that somehow have always known,
and yet tricks and games,
rocks and stones met us along the way...

Hold on hold fast to that which you know deep
within the voice of
God always lets you know...
The voice inside, the voice within...

The God in you always let HIM live within you, to
help you sing that special song,
that special gift HE only gave to you...

Work hard to keep it let the dream stay alive,
even when others or life has taken you to a dark
place remember the light...
The light of Jesus the light HE left for you inside.
He awaits you / us to answer HIS call...
HE's been knocking, calling ever so quietly, but
we're so busy moving, running
we can't always hear the voice inside...

Somehow we think we'll miss something if we're
not in motion
going out all the time, never standing still to even
hear our own voices, crying,
and screaming inside...

Hurting, wondering why it's all going wrong, stop
stand still get quite and hear HIM calling, answer
the call knowing HE's always with you. Always
watching,
and wanting the best for you, always LOVING...

Patiently waiting for us to begin our journey to
share the gifts He's bestowed upon us to reach out
and help others so that they may know how they
can shorten their road
to their journey.

As they tell how long their journey has been that
somehow they wondered and
now you can share the peace and the glory HIS
GLORY from within...

Knowing that planting this new seed within them
will allow others to blossom...
Road to the Journey is it short or long, do you
know how you can grow as a beautiful tree, plant
those seeds of LOVE that you've learned along the
way by
Shortening the journey for those along the way...

Shortening the journey for someone can potential
mean the difference
Between going around in circles for 11 days or 40
years...
Looking down the same road wondering if there's
It's ever going to change, will it lead to a
new way or just remain the same...

We all know there are many ways to get to the
Same place, but do we remain on road
Or venture towards another way...

Road to Towards the Journey which one we'll we
take?
Do we even know the way?
Will we stop to ask for help if we get lost along
The way?

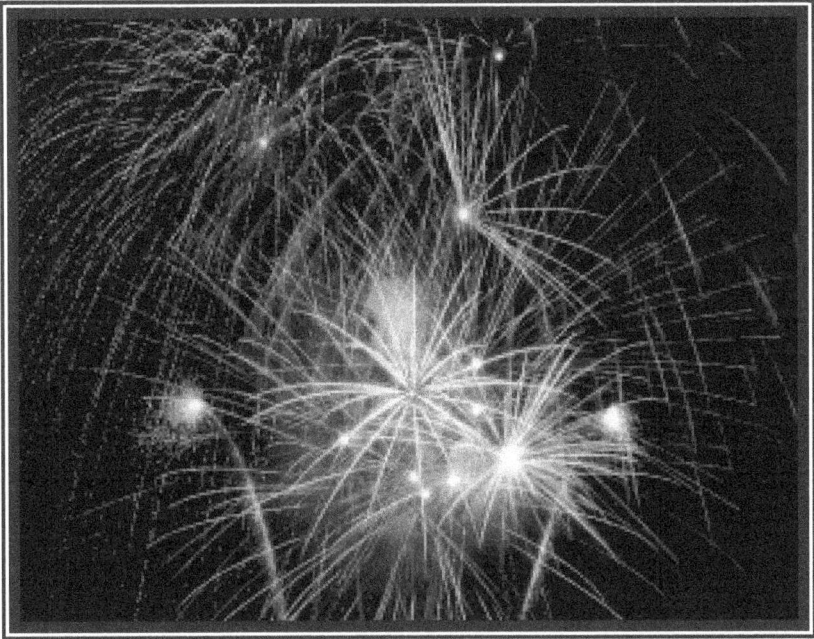

What We Learn Along the Way

We learn to stand through the storm no matter
how strong or small.
We learn to love even more, to listen a little closer,
to share and to love,
to cry and to laugh...

We learn that God has always been there
patiently lovingly...
Letting us know that for each of us these special
gifts, gifts of passion, gifts of desire,
gift of loving;
Are his way of sharing with the world how unique
and special each of us are...

And, that collectively we're a wonderful tapestry
of His LOVE...
We learn that each member has a special part a
special role to take part
Working together to make one...
One grand happy, joyful family of love, HIS LOVE
– AGAPE LOVE
An unconditional love that truly passes all
understanding...

We learn that there's no need to be envious,
jealous of any one else's gift,
But to embrace it and rejoice in another members
unique role,
Not a strange role, because what appears to be
strange maybe just
the greatest gift of all...
We should learn this early in life rather than
later.
Learn not to be afraid and know God hasn't given
us a spirit of fear
But of love, power and a sound mind...
Learn and practice how to achieve this sound
mind it can save
your life and others.
Stop, take a breath count to ten slow things down
a moment
Smell the flowers take hold of the beauty of the
world.

Learn that we are but a spec of sand in the broad
scope of the world
Clearly in the scope of the universe...
When we learn how intense that thought is it will
humble you,

And when you learn that each star and plant
within
The universe plays its own unique role
It helps you better appreciate your role and how
unique it is.

Take a moment or two to really take this one in.
When you do you'll realize that we don't always
have to react to everything.
We can stop and take a moment to take it all in,
So we don't miss any moments of opportunity to
share our story
And to really hear others, to see if we're parts that
are
Here to join together...

I know it can be very difficult with some just go
into their prayer closet and ask
God to speak to their spirit within...
To reveal the mystery of HIS word which is ever
so simple.
Yet we tend to make it harder than it really is...
Remember come to me as a child why does HE tell
us this
Because the mind of a child can be so innocent so
simple.
Uncorrupted with their hearts full of joy...

Learning this special gift of a child as we grow
into adults
Can be our saving grace...
It's not silly, it's not immature
We can still be adults and responsible but the
ability
To reach out to the child inside can be a
comforting place to be.

A place that God holds dear because we receive
better from this place
Without our prejudices, without our suspicions,
without our doubts,
without our anger and pain, and without our
unforgiveness...
Just a place were we see things from the simplest
place
with simple understanding, without our
judgments, without our analysis,
without applying all our intelligence, and
criticisms...

Learning and becoming friends and at peace with
This place makes the journey worth while.
Makes the journey full of joy
Makes the journey a playful place...

We bring this innocence so it helps shorten the
road
A road full of exploration
Children love to explore they learn so much
It helps them grow, grow stronger learn faster.

We can learn so much from children whether your
own
Or someone else's.
Have you ever noticed how profound a child's
words can be
The visions they see...

We learn that their lives are simple and free
Even the children of the world that have suffered
Along the way have stories of joy they can share
Their innocence holds their peace...

God somehow holds them within His special
garden
HIS special place, a place of comfort
A place of LOVE.

We learn that God holds this special place for all
of us.
Do we dare to go within?
Do we dare to call HIS NAME?
Do we dare to try to know him?
Or are we still afraid?

When you traveled through your journey did you
get scared along the way?
If so sit back watch the children of the world...
If so go outside and look up to the sky...
Go by a beautiful park, lake or pond,
Look at the trees, and plants around you
Listen to the songs of nature...

Nature's song quite still yet full of HIS wonders...
Full of the simple intrigue of life is in its
dependence on HIM.
Birds and animals of the world have no idea from
one
Moment to the next how they will eat
Or were they should go or do they?...

Learn how in their innocence God's always near.
Like birds when the seasons change they know
To go from north or south...
Bears know when it's time to hibernate and when
to come out...

Their innocence is just like a child they just listen

To the voice all around and inside,
Did you learn this along the way...?

If you did, it helps shorten your journey,
Did you go and then tell?
Tell your story of how simple it all can be
Even when the storm was all around you,
You stood through the end...

When Jesus called his disciples to step outside the
boat
Could you answer HIS call?
Could you step out in Faith?
Did you answer HIS call?

We pick up the phone to answer a call for
everyone else
Can we answer HIS call, a call that can save our
lives?
A call that when answered can save your life
In saving your life others come too...

2

❊❊❊

Story of the Journey

When God instructed Moses to begin an Exodus of his people from Egypt it's interesting to note it should have taken 11 days as apposed to 40 years. What happened along the way? What happened along the way are different stories we all can testify to. It's the story of our journeys...

That voice inside that has spoken to us over the years, a voice we didn't always understand. A voice we questioned even when we knew it was right, we had to have our way; but what was the cost?

It cost us time whether it's because we didn't hear the voice from within or those around us... Either way we didn't hear maybe because we just didn't know. My people perish for a lack of knowledge...

What can this lack of knowledge cost? It can cost time, it can cost opportunity, it can cost relationships, and it can potentially cost our lives... Once we know what do we do, what can we do? We can capture the moment of awareness of revelation and ride the wave, master the waves, follow the wave...

This time of internal evolution, spiritual awakening a moment so intense one might find it hard to describe. This story of a journey travailed through deceptions, abuse, life threatening. Watch that I maintained and travailed through the storm because by grace God made me aware through revelation, and through HIS LOVE...

Were there beautiful rewarding moments along the way, moments of opportunity along the way? Yes, but sometimes when it gets really cloudy that's hard to see. Situations that you'd ask someone whether they were talking about a movie or a book they read. But, even through the storms I always knew God was there keeping me aware, lighting the light when HE began to see it trying to go out... Calling to my memory His WORD, his GRACE, his LOVE, and his HEART...

That no matter how rough, how scary He was by my side, through it all He held my hand and my heart...

No matter what HE let me know we should always know HIM because his word will not return void. That no weapon formed against us shall profit, and no harm shall come to my anointed...

Moments which transcend to reaching out to someone else to help them along the way One can drown in reliving; rehashing all the situations and storms but only to let someone see they're not alone by testifying...

Yes, it can be very scary, very lonely, very unsettling, and even life threatening, but if somehow you can hold on to the light of God within HE will always see you through.

Cry out HIS name, reach out to someone who you know has a love for God an understanding of his word, and no I'm not talking about religion, I'm talking about God and your personnel relationship with HIM.

A relationship that God has a way of helping you understand and become hungry for even more... Something so special that sometimes it's very hard to describe to others, other than to say it's the type of LOVING relationship that we spend 40 years to find, when we could have obtained it in 11 days...

If you're in an unsettling situation now I urge you to call on the name of Jesus, simply call God and talk to Him, ask the The Holy Spirit who will show you how. This trinity is an awesome power God our heavenly Father who created the universe and everything within, He sent HIS only begotten SON to show the world his LOVE, his compassion, his grace, his light, and his healing power. Jesus came to show us the way the truth and the light that no one can come to the Father but through HIM. The Holy Spirit came to hold our hand teaching us, guiding us along the way. The comforter implements the passion of Gods Heart and HIS Power of His SONS Sacrifice...

Today, Monday, December 31, 2007 New Years Eve around 11:34 a.m. ironically I sit here right now needing to defer to the paragraph above. My situation is quite intense and this intensity drives me to have to reach out to God to see me through. The pain I'm feeling right now I can't even describe to the core of one's soul, one's spirit. So, I'm calling out to God literally right now as I write, please help me [for You said no more than what one can bare] and I'm so tired and yet I'm strong and I know that's because of YOU AND YOUR HEART, THE HEART OF GOD AND HIS LOVE...

I'm holding on with this amazing Strength that
God's will bring up
from out of no where, He'll make a way out of no
way...

I'm holding on because of my awareness that gifts
He's bestowed upon
me haven't all come to fruition...

I'm holding on because HIS WORD bares truth,
and ['In the beginning
was the Word, and the Word was with God, and
the Word was God.' –
John – Enjoy reading Chapter 1 KJV]

I'm holding on because life is here for us to live
and learn enjoy all the
Good, and learn every lesson from the bad...

I'm holding on because there are so many journeys
to share...
Whether they're the same or different
there are lessons to be learned...

I'm holding on because maybe by writing God can
touch your heart
through this journey with me. Maybe, and
hopefully save you
sometime on your journey...

I'm holding on because life's testimonies can be
ever so healing and
there are so many testimonies to be heard and
shared with...

Holding on to God, Holding onto Faith, knowing
that God's Heart, and
His Love is Internal...

I know some of you may have wondered what where some of the situations that led to my life's lessons as it relates to my journey. Although, I was blessed to receive exposure to culture, education, and performing arts early in life and throughout; a portion of this journey included verbal & physical abuse, betrayal, rejection, adultery. You will not see an elaborate degree of the detail of what occurred; only that it occurred but through it all I still held on to God, Jesus, and The Holy Spirit to hold my hand. It wasn't always easy but all I can say about that is that God has such an amazing way of bringing a sense of peace and calm in the middle of the storm.

While you're going through life's storms [trials & tribulations], it can be difficult sometimes to actually hold on to the light but I'm hear to let you know it pays to reach out to God. Reach out to God and He will reach back it isn't always when we want him to but it's right on time. Hold on to God and His unchanging hand.

You see, many of us are known to wavier in the mist of the storm wanting to take control, letting go and letting God and when we feel He isn't moving fast enough we jump in. Letting go to let God isn't an easy process especially if you're a take charge type of person. We're told in his Word to cast our cares upon Him, 'all them that labour and are heavy laden come to me and I will give you rest' – Matthew 11:28 KJV. Letting go and letting God will require you to work through not engaging ourselves with the situation, which at times can really consume us...Just the pain and burden of it, the overall feeling of intensity the potential impacts it can all be to much. But, no matter what hold on continue to reach out when you need help go to God, close family and friends. Sometimes, we don't know but someone around us may have gone through the same thing and can offer their knowledge or share a prayer.

We never know where our prayer warriors maybe, 'be aware of strangers unaware'. All prayer warriors aren't in church, because church is everywhere. When we take a moment to testify to and with someone by appreciating God's presence in our lives, the situations that God has pulled us through you can't help but raise your hands to praise Him.

To glorify Him, to honor Him, to love Him, to trust Him, to listen to Him,
to want to know His heart, to reach out to Him,
to appreciate Him...

3

Journey Through the Strongholds

Throughout our journey we may notice patterns, cycles, and seasons of time when it appears we're going in circles. Why, what does this mean? These seasons of time maybe related to strongholds. Strongholds[1] as an example can be something that's been holding you back from truly accomplishing that which you know you must

---

[1]**American Psychological Association (APA):**
strongholds. (n.d.). *The American Heritage® Dictionary of the English Language, Fourth Edition.* Retrieved January 15, 2008, from Dictionary.com website: http://dictionary.reference.com/ browse/strongholds

Chicago Manual Style (CMS):
strongholds. Dictionary.com. *The American Heritage® Dictionary of the English Language, Fourth Edition.* Houghton Mifflin Company, 2004. http://dictionary.reference.com/browse/ strongholds (accessed: January 15, 2008).

Modern Language Association (MLA):
"strongholds." The American Heritage® Dictionary of the English Language, Fourth Edition. Houghton Mifflin Company, 2004. 15 Jan. 2008. <Dictionary.com http://dictionary.reference. com/browse/strongholds>.

overcome to reach your destiny. Something that keeps you distracted causes you to procrastinate, an obstacle, the feeling that you're being held in a holding pattern.

Stronghold, a solid foundation like a fortress, building or house built upon a rock where the gates of hell shall not prevail, as in God's word. Stronghold / strongholds have positive and/or negative applications and connotations.

Stronghold / s with Positive connotations holding on to your dreams those gifts from God that you know in your heart He supplied...

Knowing that these Gifts His Treasures unto you an Anointing that ONLY GOD CAN SUPPLY... Embracing God's Anointed Gifts taking the time to get to know them is a Stronghold / s with Positive connotations...

Thereby, Embracing God as a Stronghold / s with Positive connotations... Wanting, Yearning to know Him, to Seek Him, to Understand His Love, and to want to LOVE HIM, is a Stronghold / s with Positive connotations...

Yearning to know Him, His Son Jesus Christ, and The Holy Spirit, who assists us in spiritual growth implementation, is a Stronghold / s with Positive connotations...

Wanting to LOVE Him as the breath that you breath, as the beat in your heart, in the things that you do, in the way we treat others and they unto you, is a Stronghold / s with Positive connotations...

To Seek Him with all of your being, to open your heart, mind / soul, Spirit, is a Stronghold / s with Positive connotations...

Understanding these Anointed Gifts He has bestowed upon you, knowing that it's apart of how He Let's you know how great His Love is, is a Stronghold / s with Positive connotations...

Knowing that these Gifts is how He provides for our destiny in life which sometimes can take either a long or short journey to know, is a Stronghold / s with Positive connotations...

A Stronghold / s with Positive connotations allows you to explore God fully, therefore shorting your journey, making you wiser along the way, engaging your spiritual senses a little faster, strengthening your faith / testing your faith seeing things through despite the storm, is a Stronghold / s with Positive connotations...

A Stronghold / s with Positive connotations uplifts God, uplifts you, uplifts others, thereby uplifting the world, you that grain of sand within the universe how Great is God...

A Stronghold / s with Positive connotations engaging others along the way by your testimony to explore there gifts and reflect on how awesome they really are. Now some may not know what those Gifts are but by taking a moment in time we can help them find out, is a Stronghold / s with Positive connotations...

A Stronghold / s with Positive connotations takes a hold of those passions of life that appear in the form of God's Gift...What form can these Gifts take ⋯ Artist, Musician, Writer, Performer, Dancer, Doctor, Lawyer, Project Manager, Technician, Teacher, Nurse, News Reporter, Computer Programmer, Truck Driver, Marketing Specialist, Broker, Entrepreneur and so much more. I believe you get the idea, are Stronghold / s with Positive connotations...

A Stronghold / s with Positive connotations take time to obtain the compliments via spiritual growth, education and professional experience to enhance the knowledge for such professions...

A Stronghold / s with Positive connotations also share this knowledge along the way. Each one teaches one...

A Stronghold /s with Positive connotations fights against the storms of life and no matter what we see our path to destiny will see us through. Even when there maybe times that it appears your 11 day journey is / has moved towards 40 years...

A Stronghold / s with Positive connotations takes those storms of life Stands upon the Rock, that House God has built of which the gates of hell cannot prevail, is a Stronghold / s with Positive connotations...

A Stronghold / s with Positive connotations looks into the Eye of the Storm and somehow finds the strength to pierce through it by Standing on the Rock and that Rock is God and His Word, is a Stronghold / s with Positive connotations...

Stronghold / s with Positive connotations can see us through what appears to be the hardest test of life, circumstances of life, situations in life, and consequences of life...

The journey that one can take can either be the 11 days or 40 years, of which the positive connotation would be the 11 days, and something that might lean on towards a negative affect could potentially be the 40 years, as a Stronghold / s with a Negative connotations...

Stronghold / s with Negative connotations tend to slow us down, cause confusion, come in the form of procrastination, depression, can work through others consciously or non-consciously working against us, and those situations, can be a stronghold / s with Negative connotation...

Stronghold / s with Negative connotations causing confusion by trying to make you believe that your gift isn't true, this can be accomplished by others questioning your decision to move towards the dream. It can also come by the storms of life and situations that can stop you dead in your tracks...

Stronghold /s with Negative connotations procrastination which is sometimes tied in with depression can be a very tricky thing. It can sneak up on you and before you know it time has elapsed...

Stronghold / s with Negative connotations can also come in the form of spiritual attacks, to identify these the Gift of Discernment which falls under the one of the Gifts of the Holy Spirit {KJV – Corinthians 1 & 2}...

Stronghold / s with Negative connotations family patterns, generational patterns, potential generational curses; meaning things like alcoholism, diabetes, cancer, abuse can be caused by exposure via environment, diet, life style etc., or generational matters...

No matter the cause when this has been identified by a given generation they should move towards Positive stronghold /s connotations to resolve it prior to the next generation...

Stronghold / s with Negative connotations can rock your world thereby affecting everything around us, shatter that which you have already built, temporarily appear to crush your dreams...

Stronghold / s with Negative connotations due to there very nature can potentially cause you to act out of character treat others unkindly, get anger when normally you wouldn't, take away your passion, your drive, and make you feel as though your energy has gone away...

Please note how important it is to identify the forms of negative stronghold / s as soon as possible. Take heed to the damage negative stronghold /s connotations can have. See how clever, how sneaky they can be, how destructive, how deadly to your dreams, to your gifts God's Gift to you...

Stronghold / s with Negative connotations have by their very nature a destructive force, and have many ways to disguise itself. This is why we must be diligent in watching our path along the way...

Stronghold / s with Negative connotations can so distract your ability to discern them coming your way...This in and of itself can increase our 11 days to 40 years...

Stronghold / s with Negative connotations are designed to take you off course, place detours within your journey, increase our 11 days... Do we not want the 11 days, as close to the 11 days, as apposed to potentially 40 years...?

Stronghold / s with Negative connotations please be aware as soon as you discern them cast them away, and reach out for Positive Stronghold / s to embrace. Practice reaching for the Positive Stronghold / s as much as you can to shorten your journey along the way...

God's Calling Stronghold / s with Positive Connotation when we answer the call... Negative Connotation, Life has us so Busy we can't always hear and/or answer the call...

As you can see Positive Stronghold /s are our friends, our fortress to surround us in life. To engage us in knowing things may not always be easy but if we hold on God will see us through.

We must fight the good fight of faith in God and all that His Heart and Love have to offer. Despite the storm, despite the waves, despite the feelings of hopelessness, we MUST hold on...

When we hold on God is always faithful to see us through it may not always be when we want Him to but it's right on time. I know this concept can sound a bit much especially if you're going through a storm right now, but know that it is. As I write this now I've been going through a storm for quite some time, but even in the mist and throughout I still hold on to God because I know He will see me through...

I know this by watching for the little signs because they may not always be big signs...

I know this by counting my blessings through life and all that he has done for me thus far...

I know this by being a witness to miracles in time whether for me family, friend or foe...

I know this because I can breathe a new breath everyday which gives me another day to rejoice in Him, despite the storm...

I know this because even in the mist of the storm I can reach out to others to say an encouraging word, and to watch their miracles grow...

I know this because HE said he would never leave me nor forsake me, and that I am the apple of His eye...

I know this because God is faithful to His word "Then God said let there be light, and there was light" {Genesis 1:3, but continue to review Genesis Chap 1 & John 1 Chap 1 KJV}; In the beginning was the WORD, and the WORD was with God, and the WORD was God...

Let God's Word infiltrate your Spirit, Mind / Soul, and Body... Apart of the instructions to accomplish is referenced with Luke 11: 9 & 10 KJV. This relates to reaching out to God by asking, seeking, knocking, finding, and God opening up unto those that seek Him...

Ask yourself have you truly asked, seeked, knocked, found, and opened Gods door? Have you always depended on others to reveal to you or taken the time to take a personnel walk, journey with God. Don't get me wrong we can learn a lot from others especial those who's spiritual journeys are further along. Thereby, allowing them to testify of what they learned along the way can encourage you to hold on and hold fast. These are additional examples Positive Stronghold / s that can get us through the rough times...

Fight hard, fight the good fight of faith to always allow the Positive Stronghold / s to out weigh the negative connotations, you know the class is not half empty / it's half full.

Additionally, this citing relates to God's Word and His commitment to you from {Deuteronomy 28:13-14, review Chap 28 in general KJV} 'and the Lord shall make thee the head, and not the tail...

How powerful these words are, what confidence and assurance God holds for us, another example of a Stronghold / s with Positive connotations...

As we compare although there's nothing really to compare between positive and negative forces and affect. Positive should out weigh negative, now we can learn valuable lessons from negative effects if we're smart so as not to repeat their use. In the end the fact that we did learn something is the positive yet again...

Positive or negative which do you choose to be with you in the mist of life's storms?

In the mist of the storms whether short or long which can you hold onto the most as you stand in the storm?

Positive or negative can you see the way clearly, can you be led a stray? Can you stand it alone if there's no one that can stay? Can you hold the line for yourself, your family or friend? Will you be able to stand on the ROCK, the Fortress of God's Heart, of God's Love...?

Positive or negative will you bend in the storm, will you waiver along...But, even if you waiver will you pull towards the Positive or towards the negative do you even know?

Weigh out the odds of which force can really stand through the storm Positive or negative...Positive will always see your way clear towards the light of God, clear towards your dreams...

Positive or negative stronghold / s can you begin to see the major differences between? The overall impact that lies within both, the number of times throughout life we're exposed...

The number of times we may have chosen the wrong one and cost us valuable time along the way. Delaying our journey, delaying our destiny, delaying our dreams...

When we choose the right one we can shorten our journey, reach our destiny sooner, see our dreams come to life hopefully shortening us from a 40 year journey...

Therefore, let's ask ourselves again when we're faced with Positive or Negative Stronghold /s with an option which one would you choose to see you through life's trials and tribulations...

Can you hold on to the fact that despite the storms holding on to the Positive Stronghold / s and maintaining faith that there's a light at the end of the tunnel. God's steered the way clear for you to get to the destiny that He holds so dearly for you...

Hold on to God's unchanging hand, His Word is our ROCK in the mist of the sand. We are but a grain of sand in the scope of it all sent forth to and our contribution to God's unchanging hand...

Please know that God does Love you and only has your best interest in mind. So when the storms of life come traveling through hold on to His Love for you...

Balancing Spirituality in Life, assist us with achieving Positive Stronghold / s in Life, thereby hopefully shorting our journey closer to 11 days... This is why God tells us to be; "Behold, I send you forth as sheep in the midst of wolves: be ye therefore wise as serpents, and harmless as doves." – {KJV: Matthew 10:16}

What's It All About Nesheba –
Ever Evolving...

Book 2 of Series 2

By Nesheba

Table of Contents

1

✖✖✖

Ever Evolving

As often as the world turns so do we, as the
universe constantly evolves
by realigning stars and planets so do we...

God in HIS infamous LOVE, PLANS and
WISDOW knew that by constantly

evolving seeking to realign by adjusting the
balance brings forth synergy...

The concept of perfection is the journey to evolve
to seek balance for our
Spirituality, Mind, Body, Soul and Ultimately the
Greatest Gift of All is LOVE...

The universe seeks its balance by ensuring, that
the relationship
between stars and planets to remain in alignment
to operate as natures source
to keep each other alive...

These grains of sand in the scope of the universe
are no different than us as the
human race, upon our planet Earth surviving for
each other...

This relationship between us and our role within
the scope of the universe is to learn how to LOVE
despite the turmoil's in life that can throw you off
balance.
Thereby, causing you to evolve yet again to
survive...

Ever Evolving are our Spirits, our Hearts, our
Minds and our Bodies...
Yearning to know as we evolve will we learn our
desires,
our dreams that keep us alive...

Ever Evolving as our planets align through
opposite relationships that make us survive... Not
always similar as familiar spirits arise...

Be not distracted by what appears to be a match
as you evolve through life.
Opposites attract to each other to balance out
nature as it recreates itself, as it survives...
As in the Black hole in space which balances itself
with
opposite force supplied by the White hole...

As in the opposite relationship of core platelets
upon opposite sides of the earth
which balance the position of our planet to assist
in maintaining its balance
within the universe the core...
These forces of nature maintain the presence of
the Earths position within
the scope of the universe is Ever Evolving...

Think of this Ever Evolving presence as it relates
to Earth and how it goes out of balance when it's
affected by Tsunamis, Earthquakes, and
Volcanoes'
Earths & Life's storms and tribulations as it
fights to rebalance itself after these affects...

How do we, how does the universe survive, what
adjustments are made to survive?
I believe in both cases we first examine our
present,
modify any applicable adjustments, test our wings
to
see if our adjustments have brought us back into
balance...
When do we even know an adjustment is
required?
Well, I think something just tends to feel off, out
of sync,

kind of like when you eat something bad,
and then bring it back up...

Well when our planet Earth as an example is
overwhelmed
By a variety of things that we may and/or may not
directly
Be responsible for let alone know anything about,
It potential can throw up via Tsunamis,
Earthquakes, and Volcanoes.

The irony with some of these reactionary
responses from Earth is
That our planet also uses these methods to
readjust itself
To bring forth balance and harmony...

The fine line we draw is potentially invokes
scenarios
which may appear to affect our planet or
ourselves...
Could these scenarios lead to and/or be considered
our responsibility?
It's a Blessing Earth our Universe by Natures
pattern constantly evolves by
Gods Design to Keep it Alive Ever Evolving...

Things that affect the Earth that we maybe
responsible for can be changed
By the Words of God, as an example 'if my people
will
Humble themselves and pray I will heal their
land....'

This also applies to one of the simplest request for
the greatest gift LOVE

Given by God. The fine line here is simple but yet
in the
Scope of how we operate sometimes seems to be
the
most difficult to deliver...

Ever Evolving to reach and aspire to this level, to
finally realize our connection
to everything. To finally understand how
important it is to get through our journey
closer to the 11 days over the 40 years...

The closer we get may very well help our planet,
our universe and our
overall contribution to it all...
As our planet and universe are Ever Evolving so
do we.

We do have a partnership arrangement ordained
by God reflected by
His permission and command
that we have Dominion over the Earth.
{Genesis 1:26-31 KJV}.

How awesome for God to bestow such trust based
on his original
Desire and LOVE for us to succeed and take care
of
The Blessing Of life
and our relationship with our planet and each
other...

We are Ever Evolving to attain this goal not only
for our planet
But also for ourselves...

To truly have Dominion we must achieve balance
within
Ourselves, others, our planet, and the universe...

Balance a sense of true assurance on how to Love,
how to reach out and touch,
How to share, how to care for our fellow man...
Balance an assurance of mind, body, soul, and
spirit...

A sense that we do have a personnel relationship
with God
To keep us on course and to bring us back into
Balance if we lose site of the goal, lose site of the
vision...

Ever Evolving do you feel you've been evolving or
standing still in time?
Have you ever wondered why you change over
time?
If you've wondered did you succeed over time?

Do you even realize how important it is to evolve?
If not, do you think it's time?
If you think it's time do you know how to begin?

Ever Evolving requires a spiritual quest with
oneself,
to truly look within and not be afraid of what you
see.
It requires us to also view family, friends, and
the environments we expose ourselves to...

Now this process may not always be pretty, but
joy comes in joy...
Remember it's all apart of Ever Evolving...

It's time worth spending to really know not only
who you are
But also, your purpose in this life and your
contribution
to our planet and mankind...

Who knows you might be here to help solve world
hunger,
or just to stand by someone's side...
Sometimes just being there with someone is the
greatest gift of all...

However not only does that person become
satisfied and filled with joy,
The universe can feel that you shared the Gift of
Love that day...
How you took time from your busy day to think of
someone else...
Ever Evolving can begin as simply as this, as we
share The Gift of Love
With ourselves we help fill our planet and the
universe with Joy...
This joy spills overflows and helps heal our planet
and the universe.

Know that by Ever Evolving you are doing your
part to save
Yourself, others, and our universe...
So what may appear as something small could be
the Greatest
Contribution of all...

Ever Evolving hand in hand as specs of sand in
the scope of
This grand vision we are apart of...

Ever Evolving with our planet and the universe
how awesome...

Don't think for a moment that there isn't some
type of connection
to it all. Because, we depend on the stabilization
of our Earth's atmosphere,
in the broad scope of its position and survival
within the universe...

Ever Evolving when you have a moment explore
some of
the components within our planet and universe
and
how they interact...

You may find some similarities and connections to
us,
reflecting how close we really are.
How important surrounding environments can be
affected by a lack of balance...

A lack of knowing the importance of one element
unto the other,
We aren't islands unto ourselves, we're more
closely
related than we can ever imagine...

Ever Evolving slowing growing, explore,
wondering,
evaluating, resolving...
Doesn't the process make you curious?

Curious to know how things evolve, the why, the
how, the when;

Curious to identify how important it is how
connected it is;
Curious to compare how many things you can see
evolve...

Our planet needs the atmosphere we're
surrounded by,
the trees, the oceans, lakes, rivers, the core from
within,
the animals, the birds, the bees, the planets and
flowers
the planets, the stars, and the space which
Surrounds it all...

All Ever Evolving some with common
denominators, many with opposites
and the role of opposite relationships are used
throughout our universe.
What did they evolve from, where?
How many common denominators are there and
why?
What is the importance of opposites attract, and
why?

Ever Evolving reaching, stretching, challenging
our patterns,
Examining there cause and effect, determining
Whether it's time to evolve...
Ever Evolving, determining whether it's time to
evolve,
you say what?
Determining whether it's time to evolve is one of
the steps
that lets you know you're Ever Evolving...

The simple fact that you're deciding to determine
anything
is the very thought process within evolving...
You're examining something about yourself or
something
to identify whether somehow it applies within the
scope of your plan...

Ever Evolving isn't it appealing, doesn't it sound
exciting?
Reaching out to change or maintain the course...
Are you on target or off?

Ever Evolving as the Earth spins on its axle,
as its internal core works to maintain itself,
to balance itself against what's above, below,
and within...

Ever Evolving hand in hand we spiral together,
Growing, yearning, seeking, finding, and
Balancing out the equation when applicable to
survive...

Ever Evolving do you now know the way, has your
curiosity
Been peaked yet?
Have you begun asking questions from within?

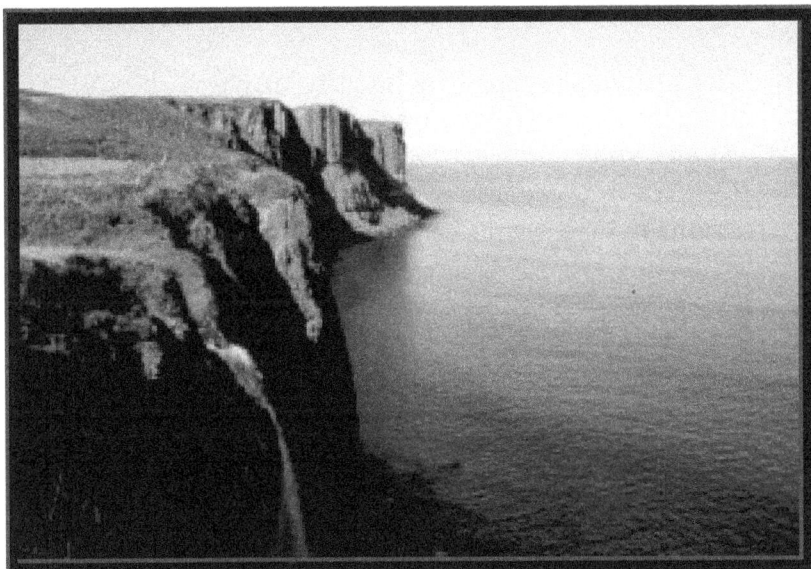

2

✖ ✖ ✖

Seeking Your Purpose in the Evolution

Ever Evolving isn't just about evolving the
ultimate goal is to understand
your purpose and then implement it...

In so doing you will continue to evolve within your
purpose to
The broadest scope of what the universe has to
offer,
and that God created you special for it...

Be courageous while you're seeking, don't give up
in
the mist of the storms...
Hold on and never give up seeking your purpose
is liken to seeking your life &
can save your life...

Seeking Your Purpose in the Evolution will allow
you
To not only explore yourself and get to know
Your special gifts...
But, it will reveal your connection to your
environment,
which connects globally and to the universe.

Seeking can be exciting, engaging, adventurous,
intense,
And is Spiritual...
Revelations can come within the smallest things...

Seeking, seeking, seeking who you are and your
purpose
in proportion to those around you...
Is it just a coincidence that we are surrounded by
certain people,
Is it just for a season or for a lifetime?

One must take this through their calculation, your
equation for
attempting to figure it all out...

Upon evaluating this equation there are times you
must
Subtract from your calculations only to improve
the overall outcome...

Some of the people you are surrounded by are
there for you,
While others may distract which can lead to
sabotaging your
Goals, your destiny...
Be careful be diligent in discerning those around
you...

Sometimes you'll have seasons when you're alone
don't worry,
These times can become very rewarding, because
in the stillness of it all
The Sun still rises...
But, seek ye first the kingdom of God, and his
righteousness; and all these things
shall be added unto you. {Matthew 6:33 KJV}
When we apply this to our lives and the peace of
God within the stillness
Our purpose is revealed....

The process of seeking cannot come in the mist of
confusion, nor by
Running the streets going to and fro...
Sometimes we think we're missing something in
life if we aren't
Running with the crowd constantly on the move...

Quite the contrary we need to sometimes slow
things down in order
To hear the Words God is trying to reveal to us...

Stillness can come by enjoying the peace of your
home, a walk in the park
Sitting outside and just taking in the scenery...

Take a moment of silence in your life to examine
what works best for
You to obtain that place of stillness...
This can become one of the most important things
you do in your life...

Life is so busy all the time, we have so many
responsibilities we
Forget to even place peace and stillness on the
list...
I know it isn't easy but please try, our health,
emotional well being and
Our spiritual life can be heavily impacted...

We can improve our overall well being by just
taking a moment.
We can reduce our stress and improve our health,
emotional state, and most
Importantly our spiritual walk...

Please find a way to count to 10 breathe, cancel an
appointment
And reschedule an appointment with yourself to
smell the roses.
Be aware of those that in this process may
attempt to
Make you feel guilty, don't let them...

There are those that believe if you slow things
down a little
You're going to miss out on something, you're not
you'll

Actually gain more...

Sometimes the ones that attempt to make you feel
guilty are
Actually envious that you have the nerve to take a
time out, again
Don't let them get to you this is all apart of your
journey
Towards seeking where God really wants you to
be...

Hold on to God during this process because HE
will see
you through with great rewards because you
trusted in Him, knowing it's the right thing to do
for you...
Call it selfish if you will but ultimately this
moment in
time is not only for you, but is apart of your
service to the world...

Have full trust in seeking your purpose it's the
most
precious time to devote yourself to, it's a selfless
Act... It isn't really selfish, it's selfless...

So if you have to tune out those that can't support
you
During this time don't feel bad...
This maybe just the incentive you needed to cut
off excess
Baggage...

Periodically, we all should examine those we
surround ourselves

with, the reason is because we may not always
realize
We've had saboteurs around us all the time and
didn't
Know it...

While you're in your season of awakening, seeking
your purpose
It's extremely important to be fully aware of your
surroundings
It's like being pregnant...
You want to protect the environment around you
because
it's a very special time; this beautiful moment in
time...

Why because you're about to birth the purpose
and destiny
God has already set for you.
Guard it with your life it's priceless...

When you truly take that moment to mediate on it
all you'll realize
How priceless this time is...
In so doing you'll note time is of the essence and
this will
Motivate you to relax, embrace the evolutionary
process
towards your journey...

Be proud of yourself that because you dared to be
different.
You dared to place yourself at the top of the list...
You dared to say to others it's my time...
Either support me or stand back while
I walk towards my destiny...

This can become the happiest time of your life to
think
of yourself, again don't feel guilty and definitely
don't allow anyone to make you feel that way.
Just go for the goal the destiny that
You've held somewhere deep inside...

Take the challenge that God gives us to step
outside the box
to be of the world but not in it...
To fly like the eagle, tiger that you know you are.
Fight back and against the doubts you may have
And know that God is with you through your
journey...

Seeking your purpose in the evolution is apart of
your journey.
You evolve as you travel through the journey
without this
Process you might not identify the purpose...

Now, the evolution can be like peeling back an
onion as noted earlier
There are many layers and some may make you
cry...
Crying isn't a sign of weakness it's a sign of
strength that you
Dared to potentially delve back in time to heal
past hurt
and pain...

In order to move forward we must heal the past so
that we don't continue
To carry it forward. We learn from it but we
should try not to

Carry it forward…
We may not always realize that these things can
and / or have held us
back within our present…

This is why it's an evolutionary process this is
why it's a journey…
How soon we get through depends on how we
address
The layers involved. Because, it can involve
mourning, it can
Involve addressing someone from the past or
present, it can
Involve discomfort, but joy still comes in the
morning…

If it does involve addressing someone they can be
welcoming of your
process to heal and/or detrimental, so be prepared.
Apart of the reason is when you open Pandora's
Box it can affect
The party you're addressing and they may not be
ready.

Please don't let this prevent you from your process
and pray
For the family, friend or foe that this opens the
door
to their evolution and journey towards their
purpose…

As noted evolution isn't an easy process to go
through, but as long
As we hold on and hold fast to God we can get
through it…

The beauty of making it through to your journey
is
The ability to return back to the family, friend, or
foe for
Them to see it wasn't all in vain and to give them
The courage to begin their journey, and by them
Realizing that you made it through it will
Make their evolutionary journey easier...

Each one, teach one that's what it's all about
sharing our
evolutionary journeys by example we all rise...
Spreading the news of our testimonies, leading by
example,
Reaching out when you can, taking advantage of
the
Windows and moments of time were we can see
Someone is ready to receive, who's been
wondering,
Who's been seeking but needed some direction,
some
Support...

Stand up to your calling that came from God and
fully embrace it.
Those around you will see and run towards your
light...
People know although they may not always admit
When they can see someone's light...

Sometimes when people see the light they're
afraid or even envious
So watch for those who may what to attempt to
take out the light,
But in so doing keep them in your prays so they
can see

Their light...

It's contagious when we go from the dark to the
light. When that
Glow is so overwhelming one can't help but run
towards the
Light which out weighs the dark...
We all come from darkness into the light and life
becomes
Much better when we walk in the light...

Thanks be to God for revealing this joy, this
peace, such love
And warmth comes from the light...
Please don't be afraid just come towards the light,
and
Let your joy be revealed unto the light..

I can't say it enough that God is the warmth of
this light and His Heart
Jumps for joy, peace, and love as He sees us walk
in His light...
So dare to be different, dare to shine, dare to walk
Through your evolution, your journey to your
purpose,
and ultimately your peace throughout life...

Thank God that you decided to wake up, to climb
the highest
Mountain of your life...
Stand there proud stand there full of joy, peace
and love.
Stand there knowing you made it through despite
The hard times, despite the storms of life...
Your dared to be different, you dared to stand
against the wave,

You stood against those that attempted to stop
you or slow
You down. And, through it all you prayed not only
for yourself but for others...

3

✤ ✤ ✤

O.K., You're Walking in Your Purpose

You're walking in Your Purpose, you've identified
The gifts and supporting plans to implement...
You see why, and understand the journey.
Your journey you can now share
Each One, Teach One...

The spreading of seeds along the way...
The sharing of God's wisdom, God's Love,
Gods' Grace, God's Knowing...
God's Gifts...

His treasures unto you bring you peace...
Bring you joy, bring you Love...
So much joy you want to share the message
Along your new journey of prosperity, the
Spiritual prosperity that guards Gods Treasures...

Walking in your purpose not only brings you joy,
But, contagious joy people will feel God's presence
In you...

Some will attempt to drown the light within you.
Don't let them disturb your peace and comfort,
God's Peace of mind within you...

Jot down your lessons along the way to walking
in your purpose. Let them know it wasn't
always easy, but once you found your gifts and
walked in them you rejoiced in the Lord...

Walking in your purpose did you shout from the
Mountain top, Lord I just want to praise you,
I want to thank you over & over again.
Holy Spirit thank you for being patient
With me...

Thank you, all for teaching me, loving me through
The storm...
You helped me find peace in the storm, that
Wasn't always easy, but I held on...

Held on because when there's no one else around
In the mist of the storm, you saw me through...
You saw that in the darkest moment, you said
You are still with me...
You said, let your burdens be light, cast you
cares on me. Rest in MY PEACE for I am
with you always for all eternity...

Because I know you believe in ME,
in your quiet moments despite
your fear you called my name Jesus...

You called out to your Father, you called out to
the
Holy Spirit, you are WELCOME in this place...
That place within you, for greater is He that lives
within me
than he that lives within the world...
You remembered being of the world not in it,
you remembered
That I will be with you always...

You remembered that you can do all things
through
Christ Jesus that strengthens you. You
remembered
That when you build a house upon a rock,
The gates of hell shall not prevail...

You felt this HIS strength, HIS greatest gift of all
LOVE. You felt His embrace and HIS grace...
Because of all this you now walk in
HIS purpose for you...

You now share HIS gifts with others, you now
know

And feel HIS passion and watch how it flows...
You embrace it, you yearn for it, you now rest in
it...
Others will ask what it is about you, I must
know...

Walking in your purpose is like a new day truly
Everyday, listening for HIS direction for
HIS plans, and knowing if you
didn't remain patient along the way you may have
Missed it...

Counting it all joy from the tears of fear and
anxiety along the way,
And yet joy comes in the morning...
That new day has begun the chance to wake up
again
To fulfill another day...

Another day to brush yourself off and start all
over again,
Holding on to your purpose to continue to walk
again...
Walking in your purpose surpassing all the
storms,
Walking and running through the storms.
All the hurt and pain gone away, now seeming
Knowing the why of it all...

Ever so resting in knowledge truly coming along,
Wisdom, humility, patience, knowing how
to listen and counting it all joy...
Knowing that with God fear must go away
Because we walk by faith and not by sight...
That God gives us the power of love therefore we
Cannot fear...

Walking in your purpose with assurance, counting
the
Blessing along this journey.
Blessing that you could never imagine as you
Walked towards your purpose...
The world even seems to be brand new and now
you
Truly see your part in it...

As you walk in your purpose you reach up to the
stars
and all around the globe...
You reach out to include your part, you wonder
how we are but a grain of salt, a spec of sand,
a star in the mist of the universe...

You embrace the very thought of it, I'm walking
my
Purpose you say, I'm reaching out to as many
As I can...
Letting them know if you're going through a storm
Here was my way out. Here is what saved me,
Here is what shortened my journey, some of the
storms
In my life...

I reached out to God and HE held my hand. HE
sent angels
To encompass me, HE placed a hedge around me,
HE
Taught me to cry out for Jesus, how to pray and
pled
HIS Blood over my life, my families' life, and yes
over
Those who tried to come against me...

HE said NO weapons formed against me shall
profit.
Then HE said to continue to stand for I am
With thee...

HE said these are the gifts that I gave to you,
walk
In them for in lay your treasures. Your burden is
Light for now you have seen the Light...
Knowing that when you cast your cares
Upon Jesus HE will lead the way...

HE enjoys it when we walk in our purpose
expressed
By Him embracing you, well done My Child...
Ever in the mist of the storms you held on to
The faith that I placed within you, you're sharing
And embracing the seed I planted within you...

You came to Me like unto a child and I rewarded
you...
You saw My Heart and its connection to you, you
Felt the times when I hurt for you, you heard
My Cry and turned your course towards Me.

My Grace is ever present in you internally and
will last
through all eternity...
Thank you, for walking in your purpose, thank
you
for sharing and planting the seeds...

Thank you, for being patient through the journey,
My Child you listened you cared you grew as into
A beautiful flower ever blossoming in this golden
garden
This Garden of Eden...

You found the fountain of youth with me, you
found
the clue to if My people will humble themselves
and pray,
I Will Heal the land...
They'll be no more turmoil, earthquakes,
volcanoes, tornadoes'
will subside...

World hunger, strife, violence, and greed will end.
Hold on and hold
Fast, standing upon My Rock Heals the Land...
To pray this pray, for everyone to walk in the
purpose that
I Planned Heals the Land...

I've planted the tools in everyone please stand
through life's storms
as quickly as you can. For My need for you to walk
in your
Purpose maintains the Seed of Peace & Love
which is
The Plan...

It takes a variety of components to put anything
together.
The same applies to the variety within mankind,
the gardens
and fields across the globe, and food that I
created...

To make everything one and knowledgeable of
each ones part...

A variety of parts that depend upon one another,
therefore
Do not fight amongst each other. Walk as the
brothers
And sisters that you are delight in the beauty of it
all....

Walking in your purpose helps to maintain the
balance
Of the planet, it's not just about the trees, the
flowers,
The birds and the bees... It's about somehow
Knowing that it's all about a beautiful tapestry...

Can you see how grand an honor it is to walk in
your purpose?
To watch yourself develop in Gods Dream for you
chosen just for you. Dreams shared then
reciprocated
to others showing how much He Loves Us All...

How humbling a dream, my special part, my gift
to the
World given by the greatest Gift that God can
bestow His Love,
His Trust in Me...

Aren't you so glad that you triumphed through the
storm?
You held on to your trust in Him. You believed
that
You could do all things through Christ who
strengthened you,
in such a time as this...

You held on to the trophy, your fought the good
fight of faith.
You defended God's honor you believed in His
might.
Not by might, nor by power but by My Spirit saith
the Lord.
Now here you are walking in the glow of it all,
The blessing of peace you rest in, the knowing and
No more wondering...

Just peace in these precious gifts that only He
has abided in you. You know that He has
Blessed you from your head to your toes...

Walking in your purpose yes each day you
can feel the delight, all the lessons learned
think on them twice...
Embracing them carefully knowing you'll never
return to the darkest side of life.

How you rejoice in getting over the plight, steam
rolling ahead
racing across the line... Running everyday,
swimming
in your purpose counting each & every detail...
Ensuring that your purpose resides in the Light,
defining
the plans, watering them as often as you can.
What
Ever the gift, the purpose it requires hearing the
Holy Spirit give
forth instructions everyday, it requires a quite
listening and
careful thought.

Capturing how listening and sometimes less
talking can be a
Priceless joy...
It can mean the difference between capturing the
next
Level in the plan or falling back again...
But, I know that won't happen again...
You've climbed to the highest mountain, you've
Sailed across seas, you looked to the sky
And saw the dream, and at that moment
You said never again...

In that moment you said against all of life's
storms
My dreams, my goals, my passions these are His
gift
Unto me...
So, Never, Never again will I take the fall it can
be
To costly, it can cost so much time...

Time that I'd have to re-travel to recaptured it all
again,
Now this moment, this precious moment is so
Priceless to me that I will always
Maintain the course from here until the end...

My drive to succeed on this spiritual Plato
Is ever so present, so near and dear to my heart.
It's like the air that I breathe; it's like the flowers
in a garden,
and the peace of the ocean to the depths of the
sea...

Come; come rejoice with me in this moment in
time,
That follows me internally throughout eternity...
Let it over flow unto thee...
Come and hold my hand as HE holds your hand,
then
We'll all walk together through the sand,
Walking within His foot print in the sand...

Hold on now it will feel like you're floating
through the air,
Traveling through the sky like birds in the sky...
Never feeling the flight as you glide with His
faith,
as children play along outside...
Oh what a feeling no planes to assist in the flight
only
God's grace and love holding you, guiding you as
You glide in the sky...
You're truly gliding through this course of your
Journey to the other side...

Count it all joy, count it all joy the knowing inside.
The peaceful serenity you can't escape all the
Peace you feel inside...
That as you create those things within your
Purpose you can have such peace inside...

Knowing how much He blessed the purpose
and everything that comes from it...
You watched yourself grow out of all the pain
To see such a beauty and how He
Guaranteed its passage...

He told you he would bless those things you do
with
your hands which came from within your heart,
throughout your spiritual journey...

Walking in your purpose feels like Christmas,
Passover and Easter
Everyday... These precious holidays which give
thanks to
Christ's journey and God's greatest sacrifice...
His only begotten Son which He gave for our sake,
So, that we can truly see the purpose He has for
us...

How can we ever thank Him enough, how can we
Really let him know we appreciate how much
He gave...
We let Him know by walking in our purpose
everyday.
Even if you think you don't know, somehow you
do,
Just remember to be silent for a moment and
Ask Him everyday...

He'll tell you listen and you'll hear, and once
You hear you WILL KNOW...
Then you count it all joy...
You'll embrace it, you'll say to yourself
All this time its been that thing you enjoyed, that
thing you wondered about and how did you just
know how
to built a house, how to fix a car, how to work
with and understand those numbers.

Oh, I'm a builder, a developer, an artist, a
musician, an
actor, an accountant, a doctor, a lawyer, a
designer,
A craftsman gee there are so many things...
It's been my passion all my life, oh it wasn't till
such a time like this that all the time it was my
treasure,
The gifts that He gave to me...

I worried and wondered for along time, but
Oh all this joy and love I feel now I can
Hardly describe it...
And, all I had to do all along was to
Stop and listen for awhile...

To listen with the two ears He blessed us with and
one
mouth to speak cautiously with...
Listening is clearly a special gift because we have
to
Quite ourselves to ensure we absorb it all.
If we don't we can miss the message which can
assist
Us in carrying on...

O.k. you're walking in your purpose and along the
way one
of the greatest lessons learned was hearing and
listening,
to the voice of the Holy Spirit who guided
you all the way...

O.k. you're walking through your purpose now
turn around and see
That unknowingly in some cases you led others to
see...
What a blessing the seeds you spread along the
way...
You didn't even notice that they began to blossom
Into beautiful flowers full of joy, full of promise...

Can you see all the blessings that reside within
your journey,
within your evolution, within your gift...
There's a beauty that rests inside liken to a
rainbow
the covenant God promises to us all...

You can't help but rejoice because it's such an
awesome pleasure
full of love, peace, and harmony...
Can you see that even the sacrifices that came
with your
Journeys were worth the sacrifice...

You made it through, you persevered, you
remained persistent, you remained
determined, you stood through the storm till you
saw the light clear...
Pat yourself on the back reach your arms to the
sky and praise
God, let the song in your heart sing of all the joy...

What's It All About Nesheba? –
Pressing On...

Book 3 of Series 3

By Nesheba

❈❈❈
Table of Contents

1

Pressing On...

Pressing on through sadness, till you smile from
within,
until the sunshine's, till you climb the ladder to
the sky...
Pressing on because it's all about the journey,
about ever evolving,

about pressing until the sunshine within is shared
with
the world...

You've learned from all the sadness that you can
press on and
how important it is. You learned how to press on
from the stillness within. You've learned how
to chart the hardest courses that no matter
what you go through, to continue to press on...

Even when the pressure was on you, you
continued to press on.
As you were exploring what the journey was all
about you pressed on.
Even as you were ever evolving you pressed on.
You pressed, and pressed as you knocked at Gods
doors, you sought
His face and abided in His Glory...

The burning desire within you keeps pressing on,
pressing on
to reach a higher ground, knowing that pressing
on became
apart of your strength, apart of your faith...

Knowing that just as Jesus says in[2] Luke 6:38
KJV as it relates to
the reciprocal nature of giving; these gifts you
share shall return,

---

[2]The scriptures referenced through out this book are from the ILumina Gold
Premium version utilizing the King James Version. Published by Tyndale House
©2006 – 2007; Luke: 6:38 KJV [I'd advise reading Chapter 6 in its entirety.]

give and will be given unto you, Pressed down
Shaken together
will men give into your bosom...

By giving the gift of giving God returns by giving
back to you,
by having others give back to you...
The Planting of Seeds Yields to others and back to
you...

Pressed down pressing towards faith, pressing
through turmoil's
then pressing towards giving & sharing Gods
Love...
Enlightening those who are seeking, becoming
their beacon of light. So, that through you
they will see Jesus; they will see the light...
You see how important it is to press on, to be able
to reach out to others
as you reached deeper into self. Press on with all
that is within,
it can mean the world to someone else...

You pressed on even in the darkness as you
continued to search for the light...
Others will be in awe as you sing praises from
your heart...
Press on, press on, and press on throughout all
eternity
Press on...

I can't say it enough press on, press on, knowing
God's holding your hand because you are
The apple of His Eye...
He knows you can make it He made you that
way...

Press on through your journey tell them, press on
while you're evolving tell them, press on no
matter what, no matter how tall the mountains
Appear to be.
Why because we walk by faith and not by sight...
We press on because He says we can do
All things through Christ Jesus who
Strengthen Us...

Press on because He says when you've done all
you can
Continue to stand.
If you can fall for anything, you'll stand for
nothing...
Press on to what you know is right.

Press on, press on let that become one of your
songs
sang in your heart it in those moments that
attempt to
Throw you off...
Begin to sing I'm pressing on in the
Name of Jesus I'm pressing on...

Others will see it, others will feel it, it will
Become contagious so press on...
Pressing on while you jump for joy as you walk
Through your journey to your purpose...

Each time you press on God rewards you, He sees
and feels
Your faith in action...
He knows you've learned the lessons along the
way.
So He embraces you with a Love that

Sometimes one can't find the words
to describe...

Doesn't this feel like such a beautiful place, a
place of?
Such assurance, a place of just knowing...
Words can't even describe...

Pressing on has so many doors to open and
explore.
Pressing on is inspiriting, challenging and yet
Ever so rewarding...

To watch the affects of how it impacts others and
yourself.
You may have never thought or initially believe
The width & breathe of it all...

Pressing on, pressing on, pressing on again I can't
Say it enough it can get you through the
Roughest times...
Press on when others doubt you, press on when
The weight of the world falls upon you...

Press on when all has fallen around you.
Press on even if you feel all is at a lost.
Press on with full determination to reach for the
goal.
Press on till you see all your dreams before you.

Press on even if you receive a bad report from the
doctor.
Press on even if you're in debt, while God opens
The doors to debt cancelation...
Pressing on to see all of Gods rewards...

Press on knowing darkness does turn to light...
Press on knowing that once you're in the light
Revelation is revealed unto you...
Press on, press on, repeat it to yourself...

Press on towards Gods unchanging hand...
Press on while you walk in His footsteps...
Press on if only to know God is with you
All along...

Press on press on as you're reaching for the sky,
the stars, as you begin to glide through the
Universe press on...

Press on, press on, and press on as you breathe
the fresh air
for it is life unto us all...
Press on, press on until it transitions into auto-
pilot...
This takes a little practice so don't forget
to sing press on when you missed a moment in
time...

With deep passion and joy press on, with love and
Compassion press on...
With fire in your belly press on, with confidence
in your heart Press on...
With joy everlasting press on, through the storms
and
the fires of life press on...

Press on like a soldier presses on in war ...
Press on liken to[3] Shadrach, Meshach, and
Abednego in the
Burning furnace as ordered by Nebuchadnezzar
[in Daniel 3:19-30].
They pressed on in faith truly in the mist of fire.
God honored this faith by letting them walk
through
The fire without harm...

Pressing on can save our life's, they pressed on
not only
in faith, but in knowing God's Love and is word
Stands true and the test of time...
His Love continues to press on even when ours
may fade away...

He watches us in these moments to see if we'll
truly continue to press on...
Press on do we really believe, do we really know?
Do we really understand? Do we really Love Him,
Can we continue to stand...?

Are we just joking, are we pretending can we
Really comprehend...
When we read about such miracles do we
understand?
Understand that by understanding what
Shadrach, Meshach, and Abednego endured by
Pressing on God spared their lives...

---

[3]The scriptures referenced through out this book are from the ILumina Gold
Premium version utilizing the King James Version. Published by Tyndale House
©2006 – 2007; Daniel 3: 19–30 KJV

And, in sparing their lives others were saved...
This seed spread along the way, became
Contagious and took over their captor
Nebuchadnezzar...

They pressed on and saw Gods reward, embraced
the Angels that surrounded them, and felt
The Anointing the Power of God's Love...

By pressing on we can see Gods glory, we can see
It's like sunshine, like seeing a rainbow...
Press on to enjoy the beauty of it all...
Doesn't it sound so exciting, so full of joy?
So full of peace pressing on can be...
I pray that you see how important pressing on
Can be...

So keep holding on, keep pressing on, keep
reaching out
So you can touch and feel the Love of pressing
on...
You'll experience all these things...

Gods eternal embrace revealing His Love.
Revealing His plan...
Walking in His footsteps pressing towards
His hands...

Pressing towards His Love, as you continue to
Reach deep within...
Deep within your mind / soul, deep as you
Reach the Spirit within...

Holy Spirit help me stand as I press on,
Press on, press on, press on, press on,
Press on, press on...

Press on, press on to watch the blessing it brings,
to feel
The joy, to feel the peace...
It's worth every baby step you take no matter how
small.
The point is taking the step daring to walk on...

Turning your back to any obstacles by walking
completely
through them, and when necessary daring to be
different despite those that may question you...

Never be afraid to be different embrace all the
glory that comes
With it. Even when you're feeling afraid continue
to dream.
Never let the fear take away from your light...

Press on, press on so that you will stand the test
of time, and
Embrace every moment...
You will never regret that you maintained the
courage to Press on on...

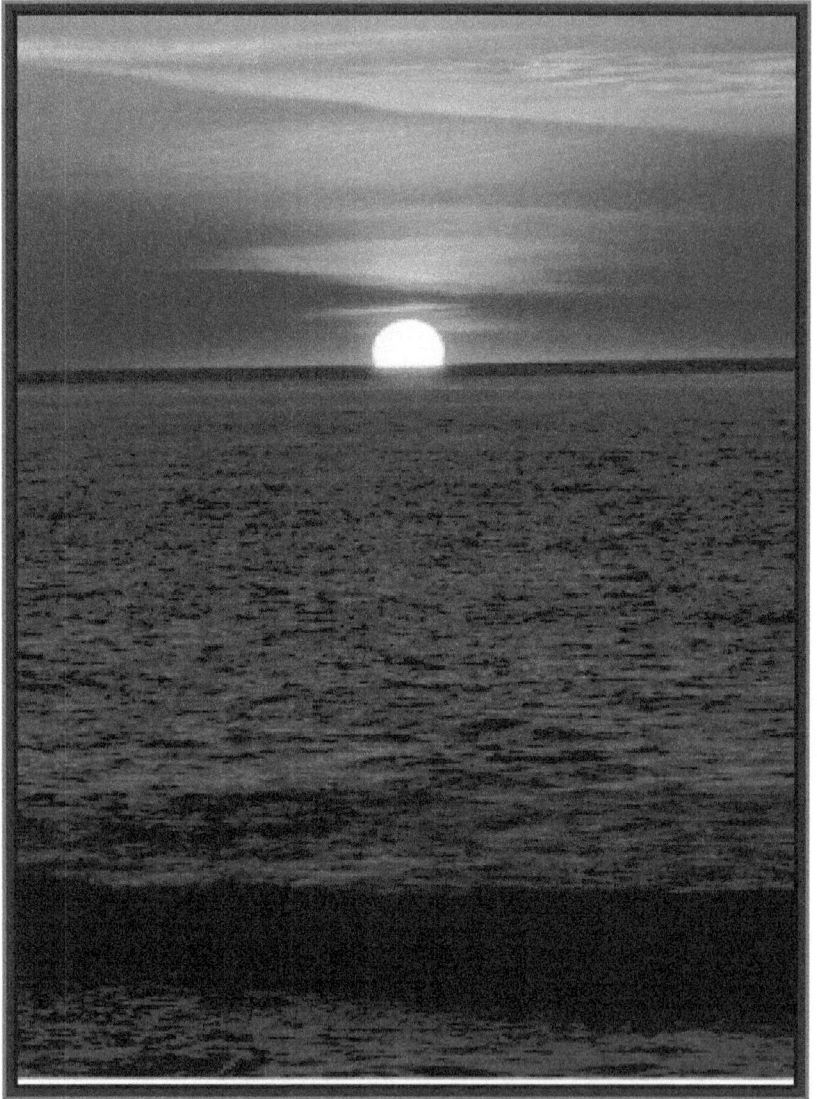

2

✠✠✠

The Pursuit of Faith...

[4]'Faith is the substance of things hoped for, the
evidence of things not seen.
[Hebrews 11:1 KJV]'
In order to pursue Faith you must begin with
some idea
of what it Is...
Faith is the substance of things hoped for, as it
aligns
with God's Word...

The substance of things hoped for, you've shared a
pray with God
for a need, a desire [i.e. continuing your education,
getting a new house},
A resolution, an answer arrives confirming your
pray
confirming God's Word...

---

[4]The scriptures referenced through out this book are from the ILumina Gold
Premium version utilizing the King James Version. Published by Tyndale House
©2006 – 2007; Hebrews 11:1 [I'd advise reading Chapter 11 in its entirety.]

Things that you've hoped for to better your life or
someone else's.
It's God listening to your concerns and responding
to pray.
The evidence of things unseen...
You've prayed for something and you have no idea
how
God will answer you pray...

Well it's your Faith that knows that He will, you
May not know how, but you know that He WILL...
HE WILL through things unseen.
He appreciates knowing that you believe and
rewards
You in-kind because of your Faith...

5But, without faith it is impossible to please him;
for he that cometh to God must believe that he is,
and that he is the rewarder of them that diligently
seek him.
[Hebrews 11:6 K]

Faith it's just the confidence of knowing that
God's Word is true.
So, when we call on Jesus and apply His word,
Those things we could not see appear...

5The scriptures referenced through out this book are from the ILumina Gold
Premium version utilizing the King James Version. Published by Tyndale House
©2006 – 2007; Hebrews 11:6;5 John 1: 1–5

[I'd advice reading Hebrews Chapter 11 & John Chapter 1:1–5 in its entirety.]

[6]In the beginning was the Word, and the Word was with God, and the Word was[2] God. The same was in the beginning with God.[3] All things were made by him; and without him was not anything made that was made.[4] In him was life; and the life was the light of men.[5] And, the light shineth in darkness; and the darkness comprehended it not.
[John 1:1-5 KJV]

When the light shines in the darkness people
don't always
Understand...
They may not understand you because the light
shines within you.
Which they cannot comprehend...

They couldn't comprehend how despite your trials
&
Tribulations you stood steadfast with God...
They couldn't understand how through the storms
God was there and answered your prays...

They couldn't understand how it is in those times
when finances didn't appear to be there
somehow God cleared the bills...

They couldn't understand that when it appeared
your back was truly against the wall
God held you up...

---

[6]The scriptures referenced through out this book are from the ILumina Gold Premium version utilizing the King James Version. Published by Tyndale House ©2006 – 2007 John 1:1–5

They couldn't understand that when you were
sick, you still stood tall
Knowing God has already Healed you
Because He made you, because He Loves you...

They couldn't understand that all the while
It was Faith that cradled you...
Faith that preserved you, Faith that blessed you...

Faith in Gods Word, Faith in Gods Love,
Faith in Knowing Gods Heart, Faith in just
Knowing His Word...

Faith is revealing to God that you believe in Him
to the core of your spirit, soul/mind, and body...
Believing in Him is truly trusting that He
always has your best interest within His Heart...

So, the pursuit of Faith is not only a knowing, it's
trust,
It's love, its patience, its understanding, it's a
Personal relationship with God that surpasses all
Understanding...

It isn't something that one readily understands or
comprehends,
And the darkness comprehends it not.
When you're in the dark can you really see...?
Can you comprehend, or will you divert to other
senses so you can see?

You will keep seeking, till you can see through the
darkness,
but until
You can see the light you will not comprehend...

We can't truly comprehend until we can see the
light,
A light full of warmth, assurance, knowing,
believing and trusting...
The light of Jesus for He is the Life and the Light
of the World
That walks us to the light...

The pursuit of faith is worth the purpose of the
journey,
The road towards the journey, and what you
Learned along the way...

The pursuit of faith is a testimony of the story and
All the strongholds you survived through the
journey...
You simply came through because of your
Pursuit of faith...

You held on dearly to your faith, the faith of a
mustard seed
at times that's all you had.
There were times your faith of a mustard seed
began to the growth...
Why because you continued to Pursue Faith...

Unknowingly your mission became Faith, and the
testimonies
of How God was with you all the time...
When you thought you were about to loose it
somehow your Faith held you to continue the
pursuit...

You didn't know why, you didn't always
comprehend,
But, you keep seeing the light which broke away
the
Darkness from within unto the light...

My people perish for a lack of knowledge, when
We lack knowledge we're in the darkness.
As we begin to obtain knowledge we
Walk towards the light...

As you can see the pursuit of faith is ever
evolving...
The pursuit of faith assisted you in seeking
purpose...
And, as you graduated to walking in your
Purpose, the pursuit of faith was standing there...

By you embracing the pursuit of faith you
accomplished
God's goals for your life...
And, the funny thing is you didn't
always know why but you walked in it despite
the unknown and that is faith in action...

The pursuit of faith sometimes you've been using
it all along.
You know those times
when something you needed or may have thought
of just appears...

When you're caught in a moment like this you
May not always take the time to figure our
How it happened.
But, when you do take a moment to reflect
You realize it was God...

Can you begin to see how knowing God, creating a
Relationship with God can be such an exciting
thing.
To be blessed to think of something and because of
your
Faith to believe it can come true, and it actually
does...

Talk about the wonders of the world, these
miracles
are the wonders of God's miracles. This is the way
God says
Thank you for believing in Me as I believe in
you...

Thank you, for sharing the gift of believing in Me
and that
My Word is True.
That I can take the foolish things of life to
confound
The wise...

That if I can take care of the birds in the air, what
would make you think I won't take care of you.
That my Words in the beginning I said let there
Be light, and the light came from out of
The darkness...
When you have the faith to believe all things are
possible,
To those who believe...
And, to believe is faith at its best, in its glory...
Believing that if you say to the mountain be thou
removed and the mountain of life's issues at that
Time is removed...

That is / was your pursuit in faith in action
rejoicing in your belief,
rejoicing in your pursuit...
How powerful are our words and thoughts...
To dare to believe, to dare to be different, and to
dare
To believe in faith...

To dare to pursue faith with all your might,
allowing
you to hold on another day, another moment, to
Hold on eternally...

The pursuit of faith what a powerful journey, a
powerful
Way of living life, daring to just believe...
Believing as in breathing air, believing in
knowing
that business you once thought of can come true...

Believing in knowing that you can do what you
put
Your mind to do, to conceive...
A faith that reaches so high you feel like the birds
of the sky...

Can you see the power in the pursuit of faith, can
you?
Feel the power, can you see the vision.
You'll know when you can really feel the power,
You'll know when you can see the vision,
Words can't always describe...

But, I can tell you one thing you will begin to feel
the peace,
as though the burden / s have been lifted away.
Like somehow the weight of the world is no longer
on
resting on your shoulders...

When you can feel this you know, and it makes
you
want to continue the pursuit as you begin
to float and transition like the clouds...

Gee, you never knew it could be this way, wishing
you began the pursuit yesterday.
But, don't worry the point is starting it today...

The world has so much going on the sooner we
begin our
Pursuit in faith the better...
The sooner we begin our life's journeys towards
our
Purpose the better...

The sooner we allow ourselves to begin to
evolve the better...
The sooner we begin the journey we can walk
through to our purpose the better.

Faith is one of the central ingredients to achieving
our dreams.
Our dreams and visions for our lives is generally
our purpose...
Apply the ingredients by having a relationship
with God, Jesus, and
The Holy Spirit and that will complete the pie...

Become steadfast as you travel through your
journey, this Spiritual
Journey, in this pursuit to Faith...
Be open to evolving, changing, and modifying
when applicable
It can assist in shortening the journey towards
your purpose...

Never let wisdom and faith fall away from you,
but
If you have just a moment always remember
How wisdom & faith got you through prior
moments...
Prior moments when you felt the touch of
darkness
But, still the light came through,
Still faith survived...

You can say faith & believing are your best
friends,
when no one else stands by you they'll always
Be there...

Faith never lets you down; it's always there for
you
to reach out to, for you to call upon...
Faith, be a soldier, a warrior in Faith, cover
yourself
in God's Love, Faith and Wisdom...

This is what fortifies your spirit and keeps it
refreshed.
Steady standing to be ready anytime we need a
hand...
Always remember Gods Love in Faith...

Enjoy, embrace the peace in the Pursuit of Faith
it is the
one of the greatest blessing in life...
The Pursuit of Faith is full of the Glory of God and
He is overjoyed when we tap into it and hold
Fast to it...

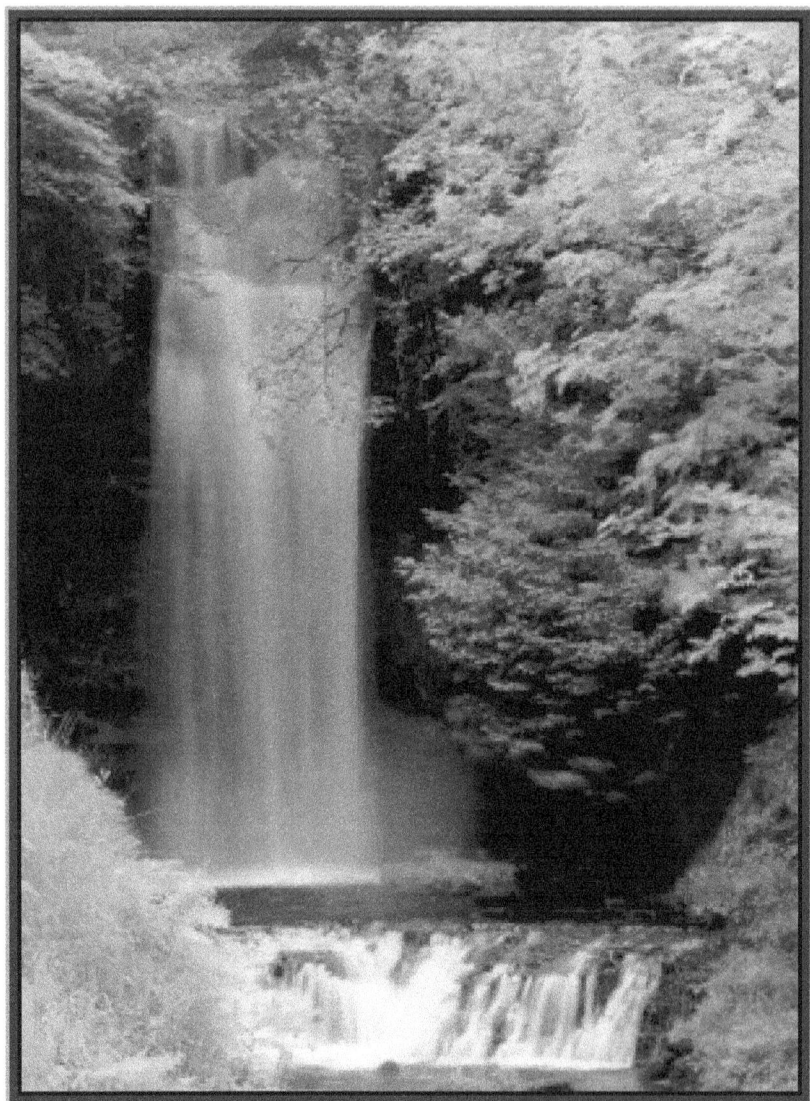

3

❊❊❊

Can You See Now?

Can you see how important it is for us to seek our
Journey. How intricate our connection is
to the world around us.
How blending our spiritual connection to God is...

Can you begin to see it now, how maybe it isn't as
Scary as you thought it would be...
Just as any new thing we might have slight
Anxiety at first but once we become
Familiar it's like riding a bike...

If you can look at it as simply placing one foot in
front of the other,
One step at a time...
One step at a time, is how you learned to walk,
but first
you crawled, patiently you crawled till you
Could walk...

Can you see it now, are you still afraid, if so
find a quiet place, take a deep breath
and pray...

Don't be afraid and count the multitude of
blessings
you already have, and then take another
deep breathe and take it all in...

Can you see now, now that you're coming out from
the darkness and into the light...
Feel the peace of the light, feel the hope, and
Feel the Love...

Remember you may not understand it all but
allow
yourself to enjoy the light,
a light that reveals enormous revelations...

Can you see now have you calmed down yet, if not
take another silent moment unto yourself...
Listen to natures sound, relax and calm down
and you will slowly see the light.

It's such a feeling of warmth and comfort to be
able
to not only see, but to realize a vision for you
has been unveiled and your spiritual eye
revealed...

Can you see now, just a little do you know?
If so, are you ready to see more?
Are you willing to expose more light?
If so, take a moment at a time so you can
Take it all in...

If you can see now you'll find yourself hungry for
more.
You'll begin to run towards the goal...
You'll begin to understand more and more
of the vision unveiled each day...

Can you see now as you jump for joy, how clearly?
Do you understand the troubles along the way?
And, when others want to wonder why, you'll
say be patient and take your time.

Be patient while exploring your journey, don't
loose hope while you walk the path...
Always remember to keep your eyes wide open
So you wouldn't miss any steps along the way.

Can you see why we can't always go rushing
around,
and why we must slow things down...
So, we can capture those tender moments of
reflection
that help us see the day...

We can't always be in the clubs, doing busy work,
But yet still wondering the why of life in it all...
Slowly, things down isn't a crime, I know others
May make fun, but are they trying to find
The light...?

Let them know when they're ready you'll be
standing by their side.
Let them know had you not taken the moment
Your life would be the same...
And, yet somehow all along there was so
much more to comprehend...

Let them know you felt like you were walking
through life in the dark, and somehow
you knew there was light, so you had to get
move forward...

Believe me they'll respect you and come to love
you more.
When you delight in telling the journey of your
passage on the way through the storm...

Can you see it now, do you comprehend how
critical
The journey towards healing and vision is
If yes then tell a friend...

Can you see now, the joy and serenity from
within?
Your family and friends will see, they'll want to
know.
They'll see the glory and feel your peace...
They'll be in awe of it all, because they
never thought it would come true...

Family and friends that have prayed all along,
Can you see their relief can you see them rejoice.
Some of them want to know more...

Can you see how evolving brings forth joy,
How coming out from the dark and into
the light sheds the light to those around us.

Can you see it was all worth all the while, out of
the
darkness into the light...
An awakening so intense yet so real...

The intensity and deep reflection leading to the
revelation
from the dark to the light...
The intensity of going within to reveal is
liken to peeling an onion back...

It can make you cry sometimes can you see now...
Did it make you go deep, deep to your
Into the darker places within, and then to the
light...

But, through it all you can still wipe the tears
away
So you can see to the light...
Can you see now?

Can you see now or is it still dark. Take a moment
to go
within and you'll see the light.
Go to the core of it so you can let it go...
Clear to your core so you can stay strong...

It may make you cry but it's worth it all because
Joy does come in the morning...
Try it and you'll see...
You'll see how He'll wash away the tears.
Remember tears are like a purification process...

Waters greatest gift is the power of purification
and healing.
So, when we cry whether due to happiness to
sadness,
Water cleanses it away...
A day's work and getting off to a good start in the
morning

or when feeling a little sick at times, water can
purify us
towards healing.

Mediate on this the next time you do any of these
things and it will be revealed unto you...
You walked in feeling one way, and came out
Feeling somehow different, a sense of clarity and
knowing...
Can you see now...?

Did you notice you just came from the darkness to
the light?
Feeling out of sorts one second and feeling like
rejoicing the next...
Can you see now...?

Slow down your day just a little so if you haven't
yet
you will begin to see...
I sense our global family really just wants a
brighter day...
A day of peace, that flows from one day till the
next...

We just want to be able to provide for our families,
Let them enjoy the sea, the mountains, the
trees...
God's beautiful rainbow of people living happy
and free
enjoying all our differences and loving each for
all the beauty within...

Ensuring our spirits walk in love, peace and
harmony.
We reach out to teach and to grow...

Growing in our harmonic destinies full of joy...
Enjoying all the beauty God has blessed us with
all around the world...

Can you see now if each of us take our moments
now
to ensure our destinies reach out to help take
Care of God's family.
He said if my people shall humble themselves
and pray, I WILL HEAL THEIR LAND...
Can you see now...?

Doom and gloom isn't our destiny, love and peace
are...
So if we haven't yet we must humble ourselves
and
Pray and God WILL HEAL OUR LAND...
He will walk us out of darkness and into the light.
Can you see now...?

When we work on ourselves pray for those around
us
And in the world, we're spreading the Greatest
Gift of All Love...
We're seeing from the darkness to the light...
And, we're so overwhelmed by the joy of it
we just want to share it all...

Can you see now individually we must become
strong
in spirit like mighty soldiers of God.
Prosperous in Spirit therefore prosperous in all
things
of God, Can you see now...?

Can you see now that pursuing your destiny,
pursuing your journey,
persevering, pressing on, loving, caring, seeking
God
are the ingredients to our overall success in life....

Take pleasure in this time such a beautiful
moment in time
is ever so present and so precious words cannot
describe...
Can you see it all now is it coming together for
you now?
Is the road clearer now, has the darkness
subsided, can
You now see the light?

If so, isn't it bright, isn't it peace, can words even
describe.
I pray that you're coming closer, and that you
have
Now arrived...

I pray peace, love, and joy now enters your life
and surrounds
You, your family, friends, and foe rest in it and
don't
Forget to pass it on...

Can you see now?

www.ingramcontent.com/pod-product-compliance
Lightning Source LLC
Chambersburg PA
CBHW030758150426
42813CB00068B/3229/J